W9-BLI-259

This book was donated through the...

Ben Carson Reading Room Grant

March 1, 2004

WOODSIDE ELEMENTARY
MEDIA CENTER

MAPS AND SYMBOLS

ANGELA ROYSTON

RAINTREE
STECK-VAUGHN
PUBLISHERS
The Steck-Vaughn Company

Austin, Texas

WOODSIDE ELEMENTARY
MEDIA CENTER

© Copyright 1999, text, Steck-Vaughn Company

All rights reserved. No part of this book may be
reproduced or utilized in any form or by any means,
electronic or mechanical, including photocopying,
recording, or by any information storage and retrieval
system, without permission in writing from the Publisher.
Inquiries should be addressed to: Copyright Permissions,
Steck-Vaughn Company, P.O. Box 26015, Austin, TX 78755.

Published by Raintree Steck-Vaughn Publishers,
an imprint of Steck-Vaughn Company

Library of Congress Cataloging-in-Publication Data
Royston, Angela.
Maps and Symbols / Angela Royston
     p.   cm.—(Geography starts here)
     Includes bibliographical references and index.
     Summary: An introduction to maps, what they
     represent, how they are constructed, and how to
     read them.
     ISBN 0-8172-5113-8
     1. Maps—Juvenile literature.
     2. Maps—Symbols—Juvenile literature.
     [1. Maps. 2. Map reading.]
     I. Title. II. Series.
     GA130.R75 1998
     912—dc21   97-46959

Printed in Italy. Bound in the United States.
   4 5 6 7 8 9 0 03 02

Picture Acknowledgments
Page 1: Eye Ubiquitous/Paul Seheult. 5 Getty Images. 6: Zefa Photo Library/Stockmarket. 8:
Wayland Picture Library. 11: Eye Ubiquitous/Gavin Wickham. 12: Zefa Photo Library. 15:
Ecoscene/Hulme. 16: Eye Ubiquitous/Steve Brock. 19: James Davis Photography. 21: Neil
Jinkerson/Tim Hunt of Jarrold Publishing. 23: Zefa/Streichan. 24: Eye Ubiquitous/B. Spencer. 25:
Zefa Photo Library. 26: Aerofilms Limited. 28, 29: Wayland Picture Library.
Cover Photo: Zefa Photo Library.

The photo on the title page shows children using maps and compasses to find directions.

CONTENTS

WHAT IS A MAP?

A map is a drawing that shows the shape of a place and the things that are there. Some maps can show a small place, such as a room. Other maps can show the whole world.

If you know how to read a map, it shows you where places are and helps you find your way.

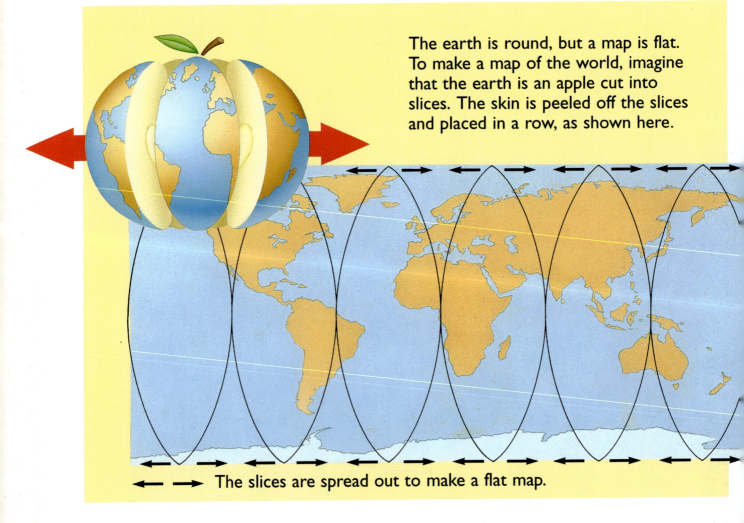

The earth is round, but a map is flat. To make a map of the world, imagine that the earth is an apple cut into slices. The skin is peeled off the slices and placed in a row, as shown here.

The slices are spread out to make a flat map.

Satellites take photos of
the earth from space.
The photos are then
used to make accurate
maps of the world.

WHERE ARE YOU?

Some words tell you where to find something or someone. In a game of hide-and-seek, you might look for people under the beds, behind the chairs, or inside closets.

A flying bird sees the ground from above. This "bird's-eye view" shows roads going under and over one another.

The words "under," "behind," and "inside" describe where the people could be compared to things you can see. Maps show where things are compared to each other.

In this bird's-eye-view of an imaginary town, see how the words "above," "on top of," "in front of," or "behind" describe where things are.

The satellite dishes are on top of the buildings.

The birds are above the buildings.

The car is in front of the houses.

The truck is behind the bushes.

Aerial View

The best way to see exactly where things are is to look down on them from above. A picture or drawing that shows a place from above is called a bird's-eye, or aerial, view.

A plan of a room shows the floor space that items take up. A map is an aerial view of a place with symbols to show what things are.

Things that you are used to seeing from the side can often look strange when you look at them from above.

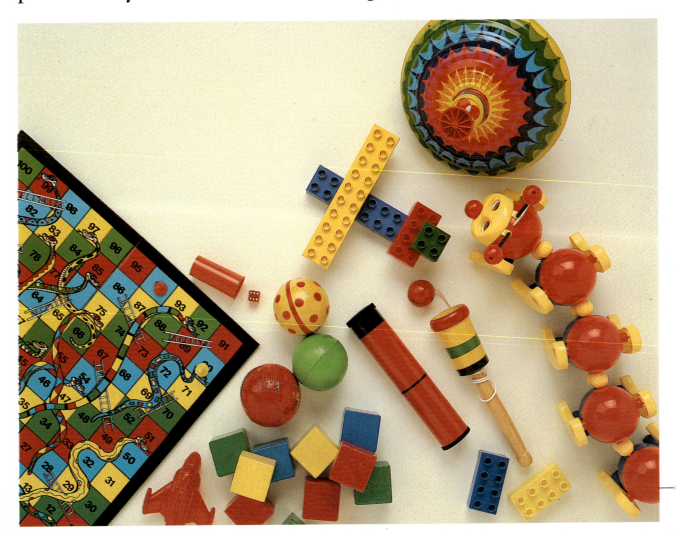

DRAW A PLAN

Imagine that you are a fly on the ceiling of your bedroom. Draw a plan view of your room. Remember to show just the top of your bed, bookshelf, and so on. Do not try to show the sides or the height of things.

Wall of the room

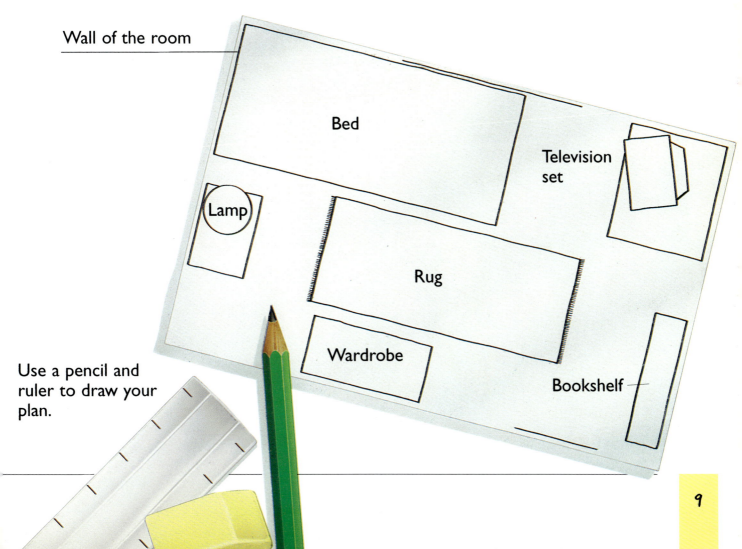

Bed

Television set

Lamp

Rug

Wardrobe

Bookshelf

Use a pencil and ruler to draw your plan.

Which Way?

If you told a visitor the way to your school, you would probably use the phrases "turn left," "turn right," and "go straight."

The words "left" and "right" tell you on which side something is. When you go straight ahead, you are moving forward.

FIND YOUR WAY

Use the words "left," "right," and "straight ahead" to describe how to get to the school from the house on this map. Follow the arrows to help you find your way.

SCHOOL

HOUSE

10

With the words forward, backward, left, and right, you can give directions to anywhere in your neighborhood. A map puts directions into a drawing.

In this aerial view of a town, what directions would you give a driver to get from A to B? (Answer on page 32.)

The rooster on this weather vane turns to show the direction the wind is coming from.

North, East, South, and West

For long distances, people give directions using the words north, south, east, and west.

Maps are usually drawn with north at the top and south at the bottom. East is then to the right and west is to the left.

USE A COMPASS

A compass is used to find directions on a map. Place the compass on top of your map. Keep the compass and map flat. Line up the map so that the north point of the compass needle lines up with north on the map.

North Pole

South Pole

West

North

South

East

N

W

E

S

MAPS AND GRIDS

Maps are usually drawn on graph paper. The pattern of lines across and down the paper is called a grid. The sides of the squares are given numbers or letters.

Things can be found on a map by finding the letter and number of the square in which it sits. Large items may fill several squares.

These scientists are using a grid to record which type of plant grows where.

Suppose you are told that the place you want is in B3. Instead of looking on the whole map, you just have to look in that square.

Placing a grid over the map below makes it much easier to find a particular landmark.

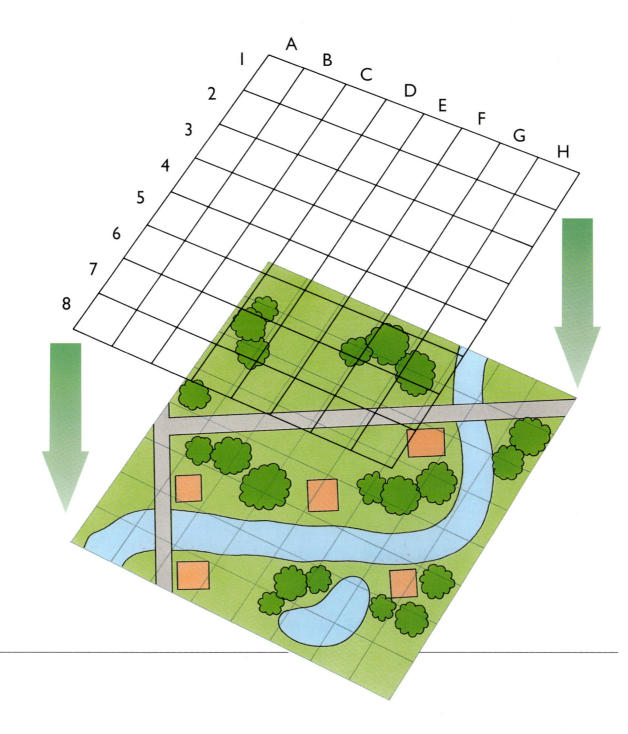

Mapping the Land

Maps of the countryside have a grid. Mapmakers use special instruments to find which places are on a straight line.

Airplanes and satellites take aerial photographs to help mapmakers draw their maps.

A surveyor uses a telescope-like instrument to measure distances and plot a straight line across the countryside.

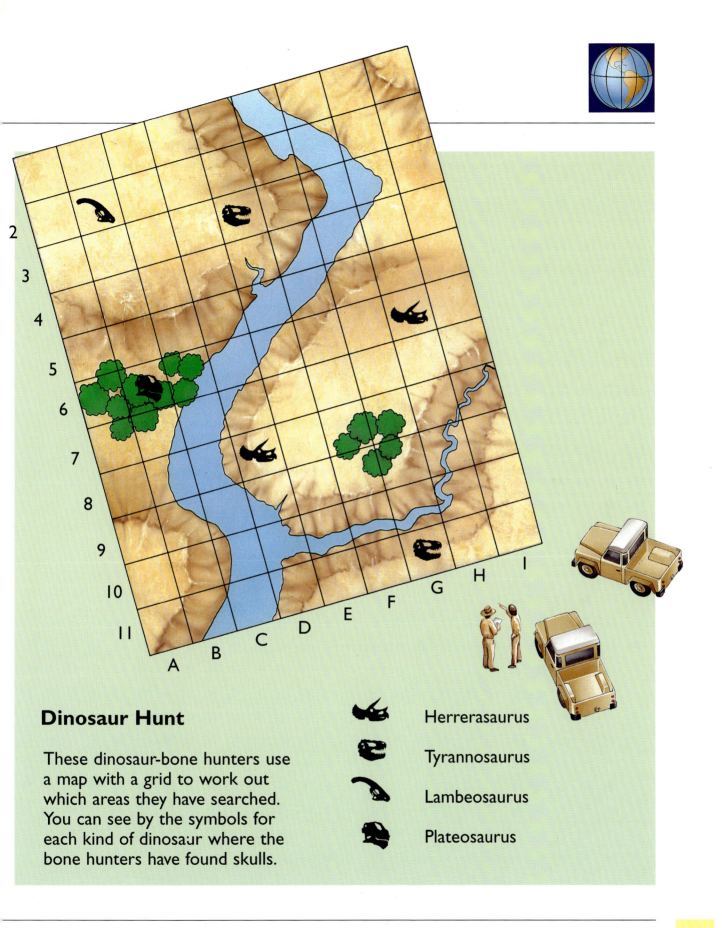

Dinosaur Hunt

These dinosaur-bone hunters use a map with a grid to work out which areas they have searched. You can see by the symbols for each kind of dinosaur where the bone hunters have found skulls.

Herrerasaurus

Tyrannosaurus

Lambeosaurus

Plateosaurus

Maps of the World

Maps of the world have grids, too. The grid lines are imaginary, so you will not see them on the ground. The equator is an imaginary line drawn around the middle of the world.

Lines of latitude tell you how far north or south of the equator you are. Lines of longitude tell you how far east or west you are. Together, these lines tell you exactly where you are on a map.

A globe is a ball, or sphere, on which a map of the earth is drawn.

North Pole

Greenwich Meridian— the first and last line of latitude

Equator— the central line of longitude

At sea, there are no signs to guide you. Sailors use special instruments to find out where they are.

SCALE

A map can show a large area, such as a whole country, or a smaller area, for example, part of a country or just a town or city. The scale on a map tells you how much smaller the map is compared to the real landscape.

When you know the scale, you can work out distances on the ground from distances on the map. Maps with a large scale show a small area in lots of detail.

This series of maps shows the scale getting bigger from the map on the left to the one on the right.

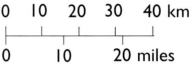

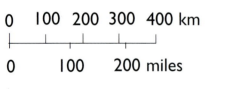

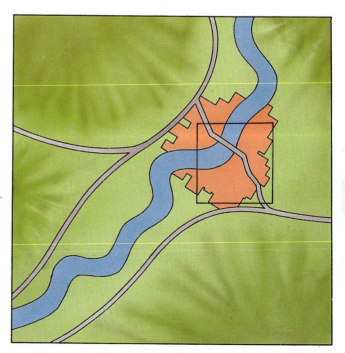

In this model village, the buildings are 20 times smaller than the real ones. The scale of the models is written as 1/20th, or 1:20.

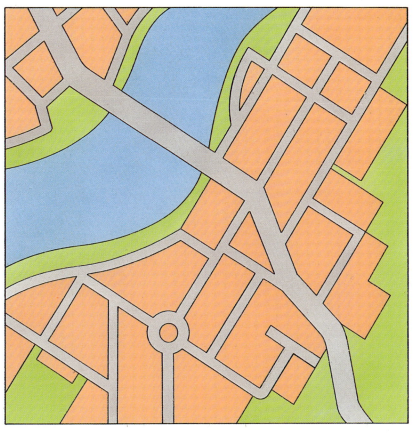

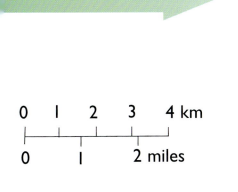

Contours

Maps are flat, but the land has mountains, hills, and valleys. Mapmakers cannot show height on a flat piece of paper. Instead, they use different colors and contour lines to show how high different places are.

The contour lines on a map each have a number or measurement. This measurement tells you the height of that line above sea level.

Contour lines show the shape of high ground as though it went up in steps. Each contour line joins places that are the same height.

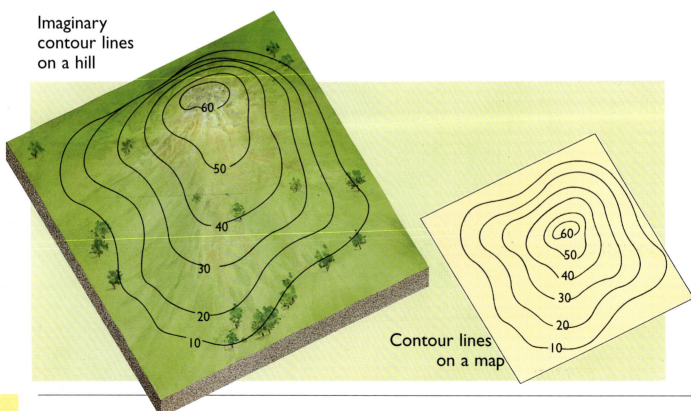

Imaginary contour lines on a hill

Contour lines on a map

These hills slope down into a valley. When a hill slopes steeply, the contour lines on the map are close together.

A map can never show you everything. Mapmakers have to choose the most important things to show. They use symbols to fit in more information and to make maps easier and quicker to read.

Rivers, lakes, roads, and towns all have special symbols. Some symbols use color. Others are special shapes.

This traveler is looking at a map of Paris to find her way around the city. The symbols show important landmarks.

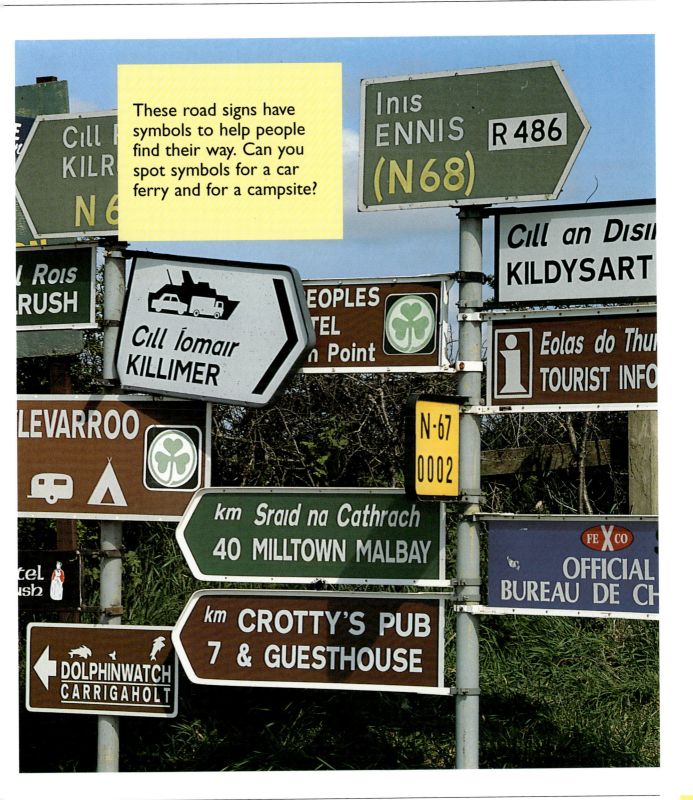

These road signs have symbols to help people find their way. Can you spot symbols for a car ferry and for a campsite?

Colors and Shapes

Symbols are only useful if everyone can understand them. A map key, or legend, shows what each symbol means.

Maps the world over do not all use the same symbol for each thing. Mountains may be shown by color or by pyramid-like shapes. Roads may be red, green, or yellow.

On a map of the area shown below, the roads, river, fields, and houses would each be shown by a different symbol.

MAP SYMBOLS

Design your own map symbols for landmarks or types of road around where you live. Remember, symbols need to be easy to understand. Think about what you want to show and then think about the best colors and shapes to use.

Tree

Railroad

House

River

Mountain

Road

Lake

Highway

DRAWING A MAP

Before making a map, you have to decide what kind of map it is going to be. Some maps show countries and cities. Others show weather or tourist sites.

Symbols on a map show important landmarks, such as roads, hills, rivers, railroad tracks, houses, or towns. Colors show water, forests, low ground, and high ground.

This girl is making a weather map. She places symbols for clouds, rain, and sunshine on a map to show what the weather will be like.

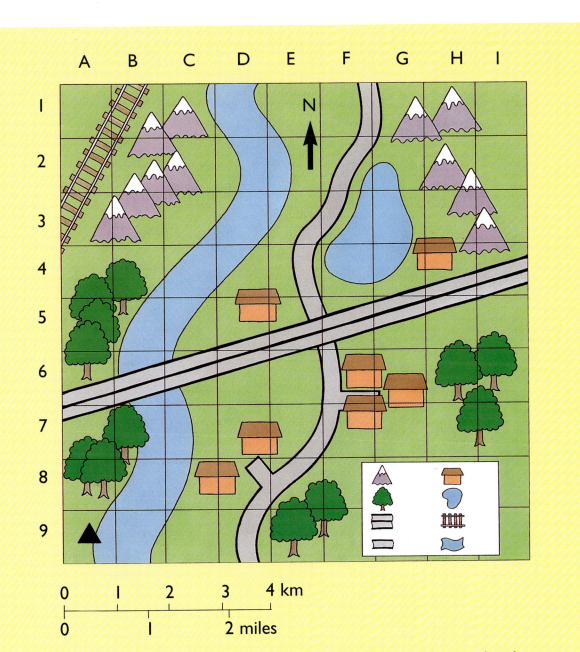

Find a map of your neighborhood. Draw a simple grid on tracing paper. Lay your grid over the map and carefully trace your journey home from school. Add some symbols to your map for landmarks that you pass on your journey. Color in your map and give it a key.

FACTS AND FIGURES

Earth measurements
The equator is 24,902 mi. (40,075 km) long. The distance between the North and South poles is 12,429 mi. (20,003 km).

North Pole
There are really two North Poles. The geographic North Pole is where all lines of longitude meet. Compass needles, however, point to the magnetic North Pole, about 1,000 mi. (1,600 km) away.

First to reach the North Pole
On April 6, 1909, the Arctic explorers Robert Peary and Matthew Henson reached the North Pole. Frederick Cook claimed that he had reached the Pole first, in 1908, but his claim was never proved.

South Pole
The South Pole is in Antarctica and is 9,185 mi. (2,800 m) above sea level.

First to reach the South Pole
In 1911 Norwegian explorer Roald Amundsen and British explorer Robert Scott each led a team toward the South Pole. Amundsen won the race on December 14. Scott and his team reached the South Pole a month later, but died on the journey back.

First compass
The ancient Chinese were the first to use a magnetic compass. They used lodestone, a stone containing iron that is naturally magnetic. In the 1100s, sailors in the Mediterranean used lodestone compasses to help them find their way.

Computerized compass
GPS (Global Positioning System) uses radio signals beamed from a satellite circling the earth and a computer to tell you where you are, wherever you are.

Pole Star
On a clear night, the Pole Star shows the direction of north if you are north of the equator. The Southern Cross points to the south if you are south of the equator.

Oldest map
The oldest known map is over 5,000 years old and was made in Sumeria. It was drawn on a clay block and shows the plan of an estate.

First geography book
The earth was shown as a round flat circle in a book produced by the ancient Greeks 2,600 years ago.

East or west?
In 1492 Christopher Columbus sailed west from Spain expecting to find a new route to China and India in the east. When he reached the Caribbean islands he thought they were part of Asia and called them the West Indies.

Further Reading

Chrisp, Peter. *Mapping the Unknown* (Remarkable World). Austin, TX: Raintree Steck-Vaughn, 1997.

Frisch, Carlianne. *Destinations: How to Use All Kinds of Maps*. New York: Rosen Group, 1993.

Morris, Scott. *How to Read a Map* (Using and Understanding Maps). New York: Chelsea House, 1993.

Stefoff, Rebecca. *The Young Oxford Companion to Maps and Mapmaking*. New York: Oxford University Press, 1995.

Taylor, Barbara. *Be Your Own Map Expert*. New York: Sterling, 1994.

Weiss, Harvey. *Getting from Here to There*. Boston: Houghton Mifflin, 1991.

GLOSSARY

Compass An instrument for finding directions. A compass needle is magnetic and always points to magnetic north.

Contour A line on a map that joins places that are the same height above sea level.

Equator An imaginary line on a map drawn around the middle of the earth.

Key A list of the symbols used on a map with their meanings.

Latitude Lines Lines drawn on a map from east to west. They show how far north or south a place is compared to the equator. The equator is the line of latitude 0 degrees.

Longitude Lines Lines drawn on a map from the North Pole to the South Pole. The Greenwich Meridian is the line of longitude 0 degrees. Other lines of longitude show how far east or west a place is compared to the Greenwich Meridian.

Scale A way of showing large distances on the ground by short distances on a map or plan.

Sea level The surface of the sea.

Symbol A shape or drawing that represents something.

Schoolchildren study a globe to find the latitude and longitude of their city.

INDEX

© Copyright 1998 Wayland (Publishers) Ltd.